#AshleyLumpkin

More by Ashley R. Lumpkin

{ } At First Sight
Terrorism and Other Topics for Tea

#AshleyLumpkin

POEMS

Foreword by carrie y.t. khoLi

PINNACLE PLACE BOOKS

©2017 by Ashley R. Lumpkin

All rights reserved. No part of this publication may be reproduced, distributed, or transmitted in any form or by any means, including photocopying, recording, or other electronic or mechanical methods, without the prior written permission of the publisher, except in the case of brief quotations embodied in critical reviews and certain other noncommercial uses permitted by copyright law.

Lumpkin, Ashley
First Edition
ISBN: 978-0-692-81398-0

Edited by carrie y.t. kholi
Reviewed by Christina M. Watkins
Back cover image by Shawn Byrd, No Limits Photography

Pinnacle Place Books
Greensboro, NC
pinnacleplacebooks.com

Printed in the USA

for Natasha Nichole Lake

Acknowledgements

Thank you to the editors of and contributors to the publications in which a version of these poems first appeared: *Red Sky | poetry on the global epidemic of violence against women* (dreams deferred) and *Kinfolks Quarterly* ([Super]Nova).

A version of Recollection appears in *{} At First Sight*; for nai's son on his birthday, at home and abroad, and Waiting appear in slightly different forms in *Terrorism and Other Topics for Tea*. For nai's son has also been set to music for female voice and piano by composer Jon Grier.

The Audre Lorde quotes used in this collection are taken from the following works: "Need: A Chorale of Black Woman Voices," *Undersong* (1992); "Learning from the 60s," *Sister Outsider* (1984); "The Transformation into Language and Action," *Sister Outsider* (1984); "For Each of You," *From a Land Where Other People Live*; A Burst of Light (1988); "A Litany for Survival," *The Black Unicorn* (1978).

A grateful bow to the Washington Post, particularly Julie Tate, Jennifer Jenkins, Steven Rich, John Muyskens, Kennedy Elliott, Ted Mellnik, Aaron Williams; and to the students from the Investigative Reporting Workshop at American University who work with them: Samantha Hogan, Andrew Kreighbaum, Benjamin St. Clair, Emma Kerr, and Ashley Balcerzak for their work in presenting a database of every fatal shooting in the United States by a police officer in the line of duty since January 1, 2015. A moment of silence for the people whose names they've recorded, and a prayer for the familes that are still grieving them.

As always, unyielding gratitude to Dasan Ahanu, Mark Bennett, LeJuane Bowens, Brandon Evans, Trey Gass, Wendy Jones, Lauren Lamelle, Micah Romans, Eric Thompson, and Chriss Watkins, without whom the words would not find their way to the page.

How much of this truth can I bear to see and still live unblinded?
How much of this pain can I use?

#AudreLorde

#Contents

#IWokeUpLikeThis   *v*
    Foreword by carrie y.t. khoLi
    Preface

#Prologue

#YesAllWomen   7
    Storytelling
    Pledging
    He said:
    Stained Glass
    Jezebel
    Decidophobia
    What's in A Woman?

#FamilyMatters   19
    Dreams Deferred
    Snapshot
    End (and Other) Stage(s)
    For Dorian
    Sundown

#RelationshipGoals   31
    A Meditation at Snowfall in Philly
    Alchemy
    Love and Other Eponyms
    Ever After
    Recollection
    Legend
    A Meditation in Rainfall at Home

#BlackLivesMatter   43
    [Super]Nova
    For Nai's Son on His Birthday
    iOS 8.3
    Bloody Sunday
    At Home and Abroad
    The Troubadour Leads the Rally
    Waiting
    For Another Brown Boy
    Say Their Names

#StigmaFree   69
    Lost Keys and Expired Prescriptions
    Diagnosis
    This is Not a Suicide Note
    Commendation
    Today

#Epilogue

#IWokeUpLikeThis

I am deliberate and afraid of nothing.

#Foreword

I want to tell a story of the day Nikki Finney reminded #AshleyLumpkin and I that we had work to do - reminded us that Toni Cade Bambara had once reminded her of the same thing.

I can't remember the date, nor the day this reminding came. I might recall the year if I tried hard enough. But, just now, those details are not what matter.

"Do not leave the arena to the fools," we, an auditorium full of tomorrow, were told.

"But the battle is a bitter and bloody and entirely too long thing," no one ever even dared whisper.

This book, these words—Ashley's willingness to linger, attending patiently to the subtleties of language, and the way they can both upend *and* be upended by life's casual ways of occurring—are a miracle, are reminder, are figurative upward head tilt in everyday passing. They're a promise of consistent going when the going gets tough. They're a prayer and a guidepost – for the going is never easy.

A prayer.

Guidepost.

… for…

going is never easy.

With Love,
khoLi

#Preface

It begins, for me, with Trayvon. With a boy who was a student, son, and friend, called a menace, made a victim, and then put on trial for his murder. With the moment that hashtags became headstones.

It is a strange thing – coming to know someone just for the ways and reasons that we lost them: Gunned down. Guilty. Chokehold. Deserved it. Traffic stop. Accident. Hashtag. Here we are. Again. Asking questions. Wondering why.

When Trayvon Martin was killed in 2012, there was a swift answer to the question of why. There was, an immediate rush in the media to portray him as a troublemaker, a thug, a hoodlum who had only received his just due. If in fact, the boy was not a boy, but indeed a criminal on the prowl - how could he be innocent? And if not an innocent, then guilty. And if guilty, worthy of death. Not a boy – just worthy of death.

It is a strange thing – being given a singular truth about a person, and made to consider, for that thing, they should die.

I began to wonder, of course, what is my one thing? I cannot see myself as delinquent or danger – but surely not an innocent either. If, for some reason, I was to lose my life at the hands of police or vigilante or so-called love, what could be the singularity that folks would be told about me? That I was a writer? A teacher? A daughter? A friend? Perhaps unstable? Ungrateful? Unreliable? Unkind? Would they remember a time that I had given my last? Or the times

I was selfish? And maybe even cruel? I have been all of that. Am all of that still. And worse. And better. And never one thing.

It ends for me, on a stage. The place I can present any truth about myself that I choose.

It is a strange thing – the dance that happens in this slam community before the performance of every poem: A host will call me up to the stage. I enter, adjust the microphone, take a breath, step back. While this happens, the crowd shouts a number of things: Teammates and supporters call hometown catch phrases; strangers will offer words of affirmation; closer friends will spout sarcastic quips – all of it meant to calm. And encourage. And uphold.

And then. As if by some inaudible cue, the entire audience will fall into a hush. They wait for me, and only me, to step back to the microphone, and speak.

It is a heavy thing – choosing to break the silence. To say: "In this moment, out of all that is true, this is the one thing you should know." It is a power that we've all held, or will hold, and I hope that we wield it well.

We have seen what happens when we don't.

Beyond that, you should know that every poem in this book is a love poem.

I have been as honest as I know how.

Ashley Lumpkin
December 23, 2016

#Prologue

i.
when the name of the town that you grow up in
is a biblical character no one remembers,
you start to view the moment you leave it as a kind of second coming.
whether school or service is personal savior to rapture you out of its small and simple,
the only truth of which you are certain is you do not intend to look back.
just ask Lot's wife -
the pillar of salt you lean on when you wax nostalgic -
if she would like another chance to run away from home.
anywhere else
is already better than the time lapse of this town,
which is all the world the old folks here will ever get to see.
when you say Venice,
or Madrid,
or even some place like Atlanta,
they hear the distant corners of a reaching outer space
and you
some type of alien at odds with the slow down
too stubborn to know a good thing when you got one.

ii.
you're a small town girl
with a big city heart
pumping "go" to the swell at the tips of your fingers.
they don't understand
why staying here
would feel like a life of suicide -
how you have already started to suffocate at the thought of not living your dreams,
how you have seen the shades of hopelessness that people settle into.

all they ever seem to do is work and wait to die.

iii.
there are just two cemeteries here.
both of them running out of space.
the gravestones read an apocryphal reference to all of the things willingly forgotten.
your one-way ticket from here reads to home like the gospel of judas.
you are jezebel
lusting after a city not your own.
do not know where it is.
trust you will know it when you get there.
it will settle into your empty spaces
quiet as a psalm
or a secret
or passage of scripture overlooked every time you have been in church.

iv.
Jesus
only returned
to Jerusalem
when he knew it was his time to die.
and you are no messiah.
just a girl
trying to make home.

#YesAllWomen

When we speak, we are afraid our words will not be heard or welcomed. But when we are silent, we are still afraid. So it is better to speak.

A Good Ghost Story

Some stories do take more courage to tell: this - I think - is not one of them. Once, there was a boy, you know. I call him a boy when I write about him, all silly and grab, and too much with his hands, but he was a man back then. Old enough to know that a word like *secret*, a word like *special* could charm a girl quiet, and we were inseparable that year. That, perhaps, a mistake of geography - of odd luck and bad timing more than predator and prey, but I found myself caught in his teeth. A timid sport. A quiet plaything. Both appalled and enamored by the rules of that game - he offered me an out once, you know.

Later, when I fell for another of my good friends, still, I saw his hands. They curved around the tenor of her body whenever she said my name; our love more mechanics than anything else - what I was trained to do. They say I suck a mile a minute you know. Gave my first blow job at eight-years-old. That, not a sad story - just how I grew up to be the girl in this bed too afraid to touch.

The boy's heart had been cloak and dagger. I learned love and shame as reticent twins. He loved Nina Simone you know. Loved too: poetry, math, his grandmother's bedsheets, the whisper of bourbon at 3 pm, at 4, at 5, at family reunions; he loved to hold my hand.

Which is to say, there is no piece of me that did not once belong to him. What is that, if not the story you tell your lover about the one you first loved - the one who held your name on his tongue until it belonged in no other mouth, who could hush you from across the room? What is that, if not a story you are sometimes sorry came to an end, no matter how sick the sadness?

I looked him up once, you know. The body in my bed still warm and sweating, like a student eager to show her teacher the things that she has learned. There was a wife and kids. The six of them stood, face front and smiling, as if they carried no secrets.

How could a public promise go on for years and call itself love, when the first rule I learned of relationship is not to tell anyone? I fell in love once, you know. With a boy that was not a boy. In love that was not love, but is still the only story about all of my firsts. What is that, if not the thing that girls are supposed to giggle about?

Pledging

This ain't no sainted, secret sisterhood –
No special sharing amongst women –
All one in three of us gathered in some dark and hidden hallway.
We have no colors or insignia,
Simplified signals or intricate handshakes,
No two-step or line dance –
Most of us are still ashamed.

This ain't no moon or candle-lit crossing –
No moment of silence or walk to remember –
No legacy of any value.
We have no papers or pearls to present.
We represent millions of ordinary women sharing the stain of mifortune.

We carry our wounds like weapons to guard what was once left unprotected.
Shelter – as sanctuary – our spirits.
Consider each first touch as sacred.

This ain't no memorial service –
We have lifetimes left to lament.
Remember.
Mourn.
We force shred spirits to mend.

This ain't no ceremony –
No attempt to take back some night.
We are women seeking daily
The stolen promise of full life.

He said:

"The thing about dating a girl who's been raped,
is she's probably a prude –
not like the kind throwing themselves around bars
reclaiming their bodies one dick at a time,
but the kind you have to crack open.

You just say,
'You're safe,' and, 'I'm not that guy,'
and the sex gets so good because she's hanging on for dear life.
It's almost like she's a virgin,
and she won't ever leave you for some other guy
because you are the one that saved her."

He said:
"Most guys I know that are bad with girls,
end up dating a lot of victims,
because let's face it
no matter how much of a douche you are,
at least you're not a rapist."

Stained Glass

The body is a temple.
The body is a temple.
The body is a temple.

The body is a temple.
The body is a temple.
The body is a temple.

The body is not
the god to be worshipped.

Jezebel

When he asks if I spit or swallow, I tell him I am a preacher's daughter.
He laughs because everyone knows daddies' girls with God issues give the best head.
We learn first how to get on our knees.
How to make miracles with our mouths.
How prayer is performance that testifies too much to happy ending.
Say "Hallelujah" when you come, and they will call you unholy,
But heaven ain't the only thing metaphored too much as a pearl.
So sex happens.
And he enjoys it.
And I think about prostitution too much to talk about with any levity because some things are not joke,
Like how I've taught three teenage girls I *know* engage in sex work –
Their bodies the paychecks counted on to keep the home heated.
And I am partly on this date because the fridge here is empty.
And there are those in the world who think that is the same thing.

He says, "I want to hold you until you fall asleep."
I say, "I'll respect you more if you leave when I'm awake;
You know the Bible says, 'Watch and pray.'"
Go in eyes open to the God who gives exactly what you ask him for,
Even when receiving is hard;
Even when you tell him to go away;
Even when you know you brought thieves to the temple; it hurts when he leaves with fists full of spare change.

Did you know Jezebel was a preacher's kid too?

In her version of the story she wanted to burn the incense for altar at temple.
She wanted to be the thing to cover the stench of sacrifice;
So when the day finally came for her to die for all God's people,
She did with her best dress on and make up on her face.
Ain't that just like a good woman?
To brave the sight of what's coming?
To see death approaching and still put a smile on anyway?
Get all dolled up anyway?
They will treat you like plaything anyway, so you'd better know the rules.

When I ask him to leave, he hears a blasphemer's tongue calling me unholy.
And what better way to absolve himself than by calling me a whore?
A thing more tease than taste, more talk than touch - a lamb worthy of sacrifice but unworthy of forgiveness.
They will ask how short the wool; how rough the shear; how loud the screaming -
Was there any screaming or did you just say "Amen?"
The word "amen," is said to mean "it is so."

And it is.

The next morning, I am still a preacher's daughter - still a Jezebel wrapped in Gabriel's skin -
A halo tucked around the things they say will send me to hell.
And perhpas, I learned to pray wrong,
But I am teaching myself to forgive.
Each poem scything the shame away from this body, offered as sacrament.

Decidophobia

When you are twenty-five and grateful for the questions you will no longer have to answer, the word infertile does not feel so much like the edge of a fist. In truth, it is the news you always thought was coming – is the way you understand a just God to be, and who are you to go unpunished? Who are you to never know the weight of trading eyes for teeth after years of walking the earth in all that blind silence? No one knows. No one sees. You are three children in to an empty family portrait – the frame collecting dust since you were barely fourteen, and you dream of them a little less now. These are no longer nightmares. These, visitation rights in the custody agreement your guilt declared between you and your God years ago when this body decided it would never hold them. And you are not twenty-five anymore.

The mothering of ghosts has changed you. You, no longer grateful for any word that does not offer a different picture, cannot imagine what it might be. You are building a language for what it is not – neither drug, nor drink, nor any strange lover is stand-in for this you did not know to want, and that a justice too. From a different kind of God. The kind that can do miracles, but often chooses not to – and you do not begrudge him that. You know well the burden of choice. The moment of joy that comes when the difficult one is made for you. The moment the body determines to show what it will with your ingratitude. It is the edge of a fist. A glancing blow that does not bruise until many days later. Far worse than it looks. That may someday ache a bit less, but will not be made well.

What's in A Woman?

When all you are taught of womanhood
is how to fold yourself in the arms of a man,
you must thieve lessons on who you are
when no one is paying attention.
When your older brother is absent,
you open the car door for your mother.
You hope your straight back and cordial smile
will make your father proud.
Your friends don't pay when they are with you
because you will be a good provider,
and you are first to bow your head
to give the Lord his thanks.

You study at the table of your aunts and grandmother
to better learn the polar opposite
of what you're taught you should become.
You're now a host of contradictions
with no one to correct you
when you learn that a man is just fist and dagger
who can't tell the difference between the woman he loves
and the dragon he is meant to slay,
and you are a thing breathing fire.

The candle in your chest burns an elegant amber
too soft about the edges to be a brilliant boy;
so you play house with the rest of them.
You learn to love your legs in a dress.
You even paper crane yourself inside
a swordsman or two,
and you love the way you were taught.
Love with clean dishes and folded hands.
You are an ornament at the elbow,
quiet and small,
even though you still hold your chin up;

brave the curb edge of the sidewalk;
learn to measure the worth of your life
by the things for which you are willing to lay it down.

What's in a woman
except the will to love without condition?
To be the knife edge of a warrior's heart
and not the thing at its blade?
It has been years
unfolding the pieces you once would not put your name to,
but you trust your straight back and honest heart
will make your mother proud.
You are a piecemeal portrait of what it means to live by trial and error -
to be some new kind of woman
and still be everywhere and whole.

#FamilyMatters

We are powerful because we have survived.

Dreams Deferred

I come from still water lake
before sunrise.
searching for catfish Saturday mornings.
If you don't catch 'em,
then you don't eat
is the joke our father forgets isn't funny
to grade school bellies gone empty to bed
more nights than anyone wants to remember.
This family is not for the faint of heart;
because, yes,
two paychecks and decent neighbors,
and church choir every Sunday,
but large hands and closed minds turn
the best dads into beast men.

I come from hide
until you know it's a good day.
Gauge the temperature of mother's prayers.
Beg the baby to just be quiet.
Play outside and don't ask questions.
I come from *yes sir, no sir*;
the rooms are clean;
the beds are made;
I stitched a meal from ketchup and rice;
our brother is tending to the lawn work;
mom is tattered pages of a wilting bible
held together with masking tape -
the words a poem promising someday
something like God will be possible.

I come from possible
is friends who will give away
the things they trade for at lunch time.
Miracles look like juice boxes

and quiet places to sleep;
from apology to relapse and sorry again;
from fear in all the wrong places.

I come from backyard barbeque
firefly lit the first day
pop comes home -
clean shirt, creased jeans and gift in hand
for all the days he was gone
and gone the days he was here.

Daddy is a preacher now.
Baby brother does not remember
the time when he wasn't.
Mom is gratitude
sitting on the front porch
singing hymns to the still water
sunshine.

I come from still water
and broken promises,
from waiting for the other shoe to drop.

Snapshot

In this photo, the two are on the kitchen floor, pouring over her favorite book – the one with the mouse and the strawberry – and no one believes she can read yet because it's the only book she reads. She calls the words in her three-year-old stutter, almost before she can turn the page, and she cannot say the word "sniff" well, so that is daddy's part. She squeezes his hand, and he calls it out every time it appears on the page. And they don't even notice at first when mother comes to freeze the day into what will become their favorite pictures, even after she masters her speech and the book gets lost in the move. But when they do, they are both model and flash, a mess of giggles and hysterical faces, and it goes on like this, even past bedtime, but mom nor dad nor daughter complain, and she loves him, and the floor has yet to earn its weight in blood.

In this photo, he is standing tall – holding on to her award – the one she got for making straight A's without breaking a sweat that year, and he did not use the word "proud" in any of his speeches. It is altogether too cumbersome to

outwit his fatherly stutter, but still
she knows he will buy her an ice
cream and that is almost the same.
And she is smiling, thinking of
vanilla and sprinkles and how her
teachers gave her hugs, and how
they worked together to buy her a
dress to wear. And he found a tie
to match. If you look closely, you
can see the swollen knuckles
gripping the parchment page; you
cannot see the bruised eye that
peered into the lens, but it is there,
in her hysterical faces giving in to
the ceremony, and she loves him,
and still believes there is more that
she can do.

In this photo, there is a huge
evergreen, squeezing itself into the
living room; the tinsel cascades in
its empty spaces, and there are no
presents this year. There are still
pancakes flipping in the iron skillet
and even the CD of gospel carols;
later there will be cards to open and
the pretense of grateful to show.
And no one is smiling. And no one
is speaking. And no one has heard
from dad in 12 days. And she loves
him, and will not forgive herself for
whatever she did to send him away.

In this photo, the two are at
opposite ends of a brand new
kitchen table. He is eating a late

morning breakfast, and she is reading from an old book. They do not bother to raise their eyes when they are told to crack a smile; they have never been the kind for easy demonstration. Once, he tried to apologize for all of things not shown in the pictures, but by then she did not believe herself a daddy's girl anymore. And he slowly finished his breakfast. And she finally finished her book. And the two left the table. And she loved him, like a ghost that was grateful for its bones.

End (and Other) Stage(s)

when you are twenty-seven years old
and your mother is dying
you are not twenty-seven anymore

you are four
at Easter in a pink and white dress
telling a congregation about the death of Jesus
you do not understand a word you are saying
but you know the smile on your mother's face
and that praise is pearly gate enough
for the itch of your tights and the pinch of your shoes
and the speech is over before you know it
but that grin is a chorus of kiss on the cheek
and hug and proud and ice cream later
this death business must be glorious
and you cannot wait to do it

then you are sixteen
waking up in a hospital bed
wondering why you are waking up again
when the pills you took were weapon enough
to annihilate the war inside your spirit
she is straight-backed in the hospital chair
clutching the bible like a life preserver
before you can speak, she whispers in your ear
the next time you think about killing yourself
remember you are murdering me instead

or you're ten
and attending your grandpop's funeral
wondering why everyone is so fly
your cousins clean
brothers crisp
you a brand new navy dress

equal parts glee and grief hang in the air
like white noise drowning an angel song
all three ex-wives are present
a taster's choice of grandpop's preference
and no one speaks ill of the man who beat his women
but taught his grandchildren how to tie their shoes

and somehow you are forty-one
in a shopping mall with your teenage daughter
she has her father's eyes and your brother's spine
which are both an unspeakable shade of beautiful
it still takes your breath away to watch her when she sleeps
and she is showing you fabric swatches
and has the nerve to call them dresses
the patterns are wrong, the colors obscene
the price nowhere near the agreed upon range
and you double over in laughter when you remember
your mother said this day was coming

when you are twenty-seven and your mother is dying
you sit straight-backed in a hospital chair
reminding god that she believed your lives were
interchangeable
that taking her could only mean that he did make mistakes
your brother is planning a funeral
you are asked to pick out a dress
the only prayer you can remember is a decades old Easter
speech
but you pray all night long

years later
when she is still here
you forget how it feels to be four and forty
all at once a marvel of space and time
there is the only the memory of her sunrise smile
breaking across the plane of her face

a chorus of kiss and hug and tears
and the moment is over before you know it
swallowed when she looks at you and whispers

this death business is glorious
and i cannot wait to do it

For Dorian

i know we come from a family that
taught us to swallow our grief
i know what it means to be full
to be empty and fed up
to consider first who will find you
and how they will file you away
how quickly your name will be among
the things we do not talk about
we are a family of skeletons rattling
about in secret closets
i cannot tell you the horrors we keep
tucked beneath our bones
i can say i am sorry for the silence
for the way it thundered inside your
ribcage until only the temper of
steel could tame it
for the need to swallow a stream of
lead to shatter the sadness inside
your stomach
i don't know what to do with my hands
we are a family of fists
we are a family that will not speak of
this tomorrow
we will bury this grief
in a graveyard already full
lord knows we will miss you
and we will each miss you alone

Sundown

Everything I need to know about
forgiveness, I learned from the sunset
in this city. How beautiful it is to lay a
thing down, even if it might come up
again. Even if it's dust and bitter ash
that frames the skyline a crimson rose,
there are still people finding themselves
brand new and open beneath it. And
we know the sun doesn't go anywhere.
It is star too stationary to wish on, but
still it dips beneath the horizon and
lends its space to delicate moon light.
The heart can mend like that – knowing
all the reasons its broken – and still
finding space to bloom itself into a
midnight, a bevy of stars and silent hope
and beautiful still in darkness. Perfect
enough to lay itself down and shine
again in the morning.

#RelationshipGoals

Each time you love, love as deeply as if it were forever

A Meditation at Snowfall in Philly

[Intro]
some things are simple
like a sequoia palm
settling itself at the base of your ribcage
its rise and fall your focus
as it teaches you to breathe

[Verse]
the butterfly fingers tug at your shirt
twisting its soft into casual knots
you are monarch tiptoe to the edge of a river that opens its
mouth with her name
this easy and gentle
sweet and shuffle
shudder
your heart an unknown rhythm
you are stained glass trusting the light to erupt
this cathedral
a new kind of praise

[Chorus]
you are song everywhere
a delicate gospel
a singular stutter of spirit and speech
your lungs filled with uncountable reasons to give this god
your thanks
while the night settles to quiet
a sanctuary of breath
of unfolding untold secrets whispering
as one

[Verse]
these things
their own kind of holy
their own kind of whole and unyielding magic

like elegant gemstones on days the simple things don't come

[Chorus]

[Bridge]
some days you are willow branch unfurled with the heavy
of your sorrow
cocooning into worship at the temple of unrequited
some days babbling brook
skipping stone
a chorus of scripture come unhinged

[Outro]
soft and shuffle
a sinking feeling sets you on both hands
your back to wall with jilted breath
your stomach turned to austere knots
to translucent waterfall rushing with the volume of
her name

[Coda]
broken promise
whispered secret
gemstone
no more
and you still
all exhalation
all night and dawn and
new day
enough
to make you both say amen
say i love you
mean it slight
and severe
and wonder
and water
and remember to breathe

Alchemy

I do not know the alchemy it takes
to make warriors from the fear we settle ourselves,
but I trust my heart is the philosopher's stone,
and this, just the transient space between us
and all that is possible.

Come, run away with me.
Let us build a kingdom where love is law
and anything else must sacrifice self on the altar of our own creation.
I have no offering
but all of me
laid before god in you – a temple
and its familiar flesh, too, a divine gift.

We have known love
as a thing worth fighting for;
it is also a thing worth peace.
So we linger here,
beneath our hipbones,
counting out a golden heartbeat.
The space between each breath,
worth defending to the marrow.

I do not know the strength it takes
to call your name above the din that says
we should be afraid,
but I have come to trust the not knowing.

I trust the things we have made on this path from ghost to gold,
and I am a warrior
even when I am afraid.

Love and Other Eponyms

Over time, we take the brand name of a thing to be the thing itself:
When you reach for a Kleenex,
you do not always have a Kleenex® -
just some unnamed facial tissue your heart still calls by name.
It's the same with Band Aid,
Chapstick,
Walkman,
Crockpot,
Pop Tart,
Google;
I get it:
When you said love, you didn't mean love. You meant "Here,
Come hold the place of the girl my heart would choose before you;
the one it will always long for;
the one it still calls by name."

Ever After

Here is the part of the story I'd rather
not tell: how every word, an onerous
labor of meaning two things at once, the
mosaic heart come loose at the seams –
weary with pretending not to be broken.
How double-dutch, the tenor of our
casual conversation. How spin and leap, a
black girl magic – an impossible physics of all at
once. How in and without at once without
knowing whether street light or stained glass
will call us home. How the not saying is a
sorrow indeed.

Here is the part about ally and always. About
what to do with the space in between: Hold
the moon like a picture frame. Like a locket.
Like light in between your teeth. Hold the
ineffable as dust in palm – poured into an
hourglass, angled like lovers into a kiss, to
make the time stand still.

Now the story: A promise and not. Fairy
tale with uncertain ending. An open heart
that is just a simpleton. Sorceress. Swordsman.
Just a girl. A staccato breath of silent longing
and how she wanders home.

Recollection

Our relationship was gas stations and waffle houses;
midnight highways and country songs;
sex in the shower at 3 am
to prolong the time between nightmares.
I think of you only with a wood-tipped black in my fingers,
burning your figure in the back of my throat –
I miss you
like a gun in my mouth.

Legend

And what of Icarus, who wanted to touch what
had once been so unknowable? To say, "This is
how I am thankful for what you have done with
all this light. I too am celestial body, heavy dust
and so much gravity, but I could be the moon if
you would teach me how to shine?" And he
reached with sweat and elbow to love the ineffable.
The sea beneath him a warning cry, laden with
bones of better men who fell beneath the horizon.
A love like this – futile, precious, destined to break
the heart that holds it – is a business of never
learning to let go. Of believing that sun is somehow
tangible, even when standing, while melting beneath
it. When even as you're all wax and brittle spark,
you are grateful to have once been warm.

A Meditation in Rainfall at Home

i am not one for bold promise
but yes
you can fall into me
make of this skeleton a hiding place to dust the dark from
your bones
i am steady now
a well of wonder
a country come undone at the hip who loves her mother
tongue
and how you speak its slang
there is no bottom here
no crash landing
no rock to crumble into
just the sweet catch and kiss of drifting safe into all this yes
this now
this cup of blessing
this
i have never told you

how the first time i heard you speak my heart shrugged and
fell open
knowing that for you there would always be room
come in to all of this wanting
i have hung your name by the door

#BlackLivesMatter

For we have been socialized to respect fear more than our own need for language and definition, and while we wait in silence for that final luxury of fearlessness, the weight of that silence will choke us.

[Super]Nova

The problem, simply stated, is one of fear, if the eye assigns color its own weight. When the body is brown, it carries a gravity only assigned to dark things. Don't a black hole collapse even the light that wishes to escape it? Ain't it a mass of physics that everyone teaches but no one understands?

It should try to be a more organized explosion, more graceful electron, and star, and matter; and ain't that the point anyway? The lines you've drawn across the sky to declare who breaks the balance here – who sends your hands to the car lock at daylight, and why you can understand any boy gunned down for any reason not offered after the fact, and what it means to need no excuse.

To know when you say *afraid*, an entire country will understand how – even unarmed and begging – the body was heavy enough to pull at the trigger finger. How – even with body collapsed – the burden of proof was unable to escape. And ain't that the point as well? How quickly you sink into explanation of how the body called to be broken.

It was thief. It was thug. It was cause for self-defense. It was crazy enough to believe that open palms are not a weapon, but how could they be – as dark as they are – anything but violence waiting to happen? Ain't that the burden of gravity calling the death knell down this side of heaven?

When the body is brown, it is event horizon by virtue of its breathing. A constellation carving out its own space in the heavens. The problem, is any celestial body denying our right to be, but know when you collapse a star, it burns back a brighter galaxy.

For Nai's Son on His Birthday

the day may come when the hounds are sent to lick the
brown from off your skin
to steal the fire from beneath your eyes
to pull the truth from your throat
do not fear
remember who you are
remember you chose your own name
you are hurricane
and hustle hard
with love enough to clench your teeth
you are cayenne pepper
and ginger root
this heritage don't come easy
you are warrior and hip hop gospel
you soldier and sound until the sun come
do not let them quiet your music
a prophet was made to sing
and for the days the song gets heavy
remember your mother is ocean and psalm
she is still water quick tongue
with a mean right hook
she is law and lawless when it comes to this heart
you are two sides of a coin picked up for good luck
you make your own fortune here
remember to breathe
remember to pray
remember these days are touch and go
remember this poem
how it come from the stars that brew inside your belly
be a galaxy
a courageous heart
be peace and protest till the lightning fall
be a light to this world
we welcome you

iOS 8.3: A pictorial discourse on what it means to say #AllLivesMatter

But never yet could I find that a black had uttered a thought above the level of plain narration; never seen even an elementary trait of painting or sculpture. In music…whether they will be equal to the composition of a more extensive run of melody, or of a complicated harmony is yet to be proved. Among the blacks is misery enough, God knows, but no poetry. Love is the peculiar oestrum of the poet. Their love is ardent, but it kindles the sense only, not the imagination. Love seems with them to be more an eager desire, than a tender delicate mixture of sentiment and sensation.
Thomas Jefferson, Notes on the State of Virginia

1.
Black people don't swim.
Black people don't skydive.
Don't go camping; don't skip church.
What is Black if not some list of things
we are not allowed to do?

2.
It is grammatically irresponsible
to call things synonyms, just to
enable an old school of thought;
however, "permission" is still misnomered
"ability" whenever the mood may suit.

3.
Centuries after all this advancing, still
we return to a singular question:
What, if anything, is the Black capable
of doing?

4.
If every emoji is its own flag, staking
out some kind of representation,
here is the list of things we have
found the space to do:

We can now surf, or ski, or be
horse jockeys, ride our bikes,
and paint our nails.
But not build families,
Not hold lovers,
Not love.
Not our purview. Still.

5.
And yes they are just emojis.
Just symbols.
Just digital iconography.
Just iconic.
Just the first time we could
send ourselves smiling and not
use the moon or a monkey –
could see ourselves as human
and watch the whole world
know it.

6.
It is combinatorically irresponsible
to include the whole scope of
human possibility; the data file
would be enormous; thus, some
realities must be left out:
The decision to include four
mailboxes – deliberate
To not allow Black love –
the same.

7.
The subtlety of erasure
when it is called universal
presents itself as new subject
with new singular question:

Why aren't you satisfied with that
which has been given?

8.
We have given enough.
Which is to say:
You have seen what happens
when we decide to start taking.

Bloody Sunday

The thing no one remembers about Bloody Sunday, is the day before was just Saturday night – a few colored folks gathered in the living room to discuss the walk they would take the next day. Amelia fried the kind of catfish that could only come from east Savannah, while Coretta stirred the collard pot just enough to fold the vinegar in. Martin told jokes at the kitchen table 'til folks stopped sipping their lemonade, afraid that the laughter would transform the mouth into some kind of water hose. Nina got to singing, the way she did – that New Negro Classic music 'til Bayard stood and taught them all a new freedom shuffle. And it went on like that – the kids in the corner – mimicking their aunts and uncles' games 'til the quiet hush of a righteous movement lulled them off to sleep.

At sunrise, they enjoyed leftovers and grits. Everyone fought for the chance to say grace, knowing this might be the last opportunity to lead their friends in prayer – to go to God for the rights they'd all been seeking, but mostly the right to meet again and eat and laugh the way they had done just the night before. Because Selma wasn't a buzzword yet for everything that is wrong in this country, just a place where Martin III watched his daddy play the dozens with a group of folks who would never dream of calling him Dr. King – not even the boys on the front porch with the shotguns cocked and ready leaning in to the front door to ask for more biscuits and tea.

And yes, a photograph transformed a nation to the kind that cared about colored bodies, but the thing no one says about Bloody Sunday is that night, the movement was a waiting room – a hushed murmur making the decision to soon march again – even while the cute boy from Tuskegee sat at Amelia's hospital bedside, humming some Marvin Gaye

along with We Shall Overcome. And no one knows which
song it was that lulled her back to consciousness, her face
still swollen and bruised from where the concrete kissed her
stubborn cheek – pressed warm as autumn leaves beneath a
loaded Billy club until the rubble of shattered bones
crunched like branches underfoot.

She married that boy a few years later, but only because he
marched that Tuesday, then came to tell the story of how
some girl brought chicken and cornbread. They all
pretended to love it because they were too tired to say it
wasn't seasoned right and at least they hadn't lost their taste
buds back on Edmund Pettus Bridge, where so many things
did get left behind. Most folks who made it to dinner that
Saturday did not make it out of the movement alive, or at
least without watching their best friends' funerals while the
boys from the front door watched their backs, and didn't
that miss the point of it all – to give the whole of their lives
to that struggle and still owe their grief as well? Still owe
their pride and uplifted heads at a time when they should
only be asked to weep?

And isn't that what we mean now to say that Black Lives
Matter? Not just the dead ones? But the ones that are one
day laughing and the next standing at a hospital door, or jail
cell, or cemetery thinking, "My God, where did it all go?"
The thing no one knows about Bloody Sunday is the day
before was just Saturday night. Just friends so in love with
each other's laughter, they fought for each other's lives.

At Home and Abroad

if he is a muslim
your task is easy
call him a terrorist
and nothing more
we will ask no questions when you lift some turban as flag
while stumbling around an uncomfortable name
keep silent
when you put his qur'an to the flame
this is what we do with faith here
make a death sentence out of scripture
say *jihad* enough
and people forget words like *inquisition* or *crusade*

just look at the brown of him
a sun-scorched desert poised perfect for retaliation
the way his beard makes a secret of his mouth
further proof he cannot be trusted
post his picture on CNN
we will see the twin towers fall again in his pupils
watch tears floating like rubble to make a ground zero of his chin
if he is a muslim
your work is done for you
a bit more involved if he is not

the next best culprit of course is a black man
with hardened eyes and absent grin
we will ask no questions
when you lift photographs of his friends
each with their own uncomfortable names
to use as a backdrop of evidence for any further accusations
this is what we do with perception here
take a color and make it criminal
say *hoodlum* enough

and people forget a group of boys can be any other thing

just look at the brown of him
a mahogany wind that whispers violent streak
the smooth of his stature further proof that he is beyond your reach
post his video on youtube we'll hear LA rioting in his speech
a firestorm of window crash beneath the hue of ebony
if he is a black man
we have already posed him angry enough for this

perhaps even still
he could be latino
an unknown country in the roll of his tongue
we will ask no questions
when you lift his citizenship
without even bothering to mention his name
to use as a reminder that he should not be here in the first place
this is what we do with land here
draw lines in the sand and call that ownership
say *illegal* enough
and people forget the crime of manifest destiny

look at the brown of him
a riverbed cracking beneath the midday sun
a family fortune constructed on the landscape of drug money
post a soundbite on Fox news
we will hear our livelihood taken away
if he is latino
he is probably foreign enough for this

but if he is a mild-mannered student
at the top of his class

suit and tie
with the promise of better things
the american dream
glowing beneath the pallor of his skin
if he is a white boy
we will hush truth into the quiet of our fear
it must be a stress response
he must have been bullied
or something broken in the parenting
people like him
don't do things like this

don't blow up buildings in oklahoma
or open fire at public schools
or invite their friends to dinner to watch another man hang and burn
they do not show up at a midnight showing to prove how dark a night can get
this boy is america
you said the other is what we should fear
you said every killer the color of innocence is by nature innocent still
while the brown boy decomposing
must have brought it on himself
antonio montes: history with police
husein suiheada: fit the description
vonderrit meyers: no angel
no weapon, no charges, no trial
no justice

if he is a person of color
call him gone
and nothing more

The Troubadour Leads the Rally

This heart of mine is filled to bursting, wanting to write you a love a poem. My pen however won't craft one now that Tamir went and got murdered. Got shot down in the street like a bad gangster film, over what should have been a good day in the park, and yet I'm all strung out – wanting to play you a radiant love song – at half volume of course, as Jordan will tell you a rattling bass will bring out the wolves. Bring out the catch and kill in a man, and I'm here, finding a word for desire to name the urgent call of my spine, even with boys face down in the train station trying to pull the new year to sun rise. How can I love you with this broken heart, red eyes, and wringing hands? What left while knowing our children will be used for target practice?

What left except these poems? This heart held in my hands? Except teaching ourselves to love after being wounded? Even with Renisha, Michael, Jonathan, Sean – all made spirit before outgrowing the flesh – this way I still choose to hold you is my only remaining resistance. For all this light gone stolen, I love harder.

Love harder. While I still can.

Waiting

There is nothing so much like a store-bought heartbeat to remind us what living is not. The almost-crimson pulling half-speed to break at the river's edge doesn't flow quick like thunder from chamber to chamber saying something like, "move or die." There is no pulse. No force. No kickback of the gun blast baring target practice on our own lungs. The prosthetic pumping gives blood to the body, then sharpens the body's taste for blood. The twist of the iron gone copper at the mouth; the language not as clear. Are you still speaking Lord? Your people got death on the brain.

They've got pride tucked open in the folds of the mouth to spew lies like old tobacco. There is a violent churning in the pit of our bellies, and this is the thing that moves us. The fear of time and timelessness got us knuckled about the throat now; we are a people brought down to our knees and altogether unashamed to pray. Are you listening?

We are as loud as the silence from the ricochet fire of gun talk. We know to shoot first; shoot next; ask questions maybe never. The answers circling about our feet will never take root in our bones, and still we press for money, power, and the right to say our god came correct. We bought a war drum and put our veins to it. We flow heavy like desert sand. Are you watching us make a mess of it? Are you too much God to intervene?

We cry holy – our tears an impulse while we wait for earnest grieving. The quick draw of our passion is as automated as breath; there is no thought here – no truth.

There is nothing so much like a store bought youth to remind us what living may cost. The blind devotion lessens the pain, then heightens the tolerance of the body. The sliver

of copper gone steel at the mouth; the intention not as clear.
Why aren't you screaming Lord? Your people got death on
the brain.

They've got greed laid open at the corners of the mouth to
spew lies like some kind of potion. We are all drunk now, as
unsteady as children struggling through our first steps. We
are wading through waters gone murky with our deception.
We forward through the worst of it. We bought a lie and put
our nerves to it. Are you watching us make a joke of you?
Are you too much God to control us?

We cry bloody and broken from knowing only an
inauthentic heartbeat. Lord, we are wondering
about this promise that may not soon enough come. We
need our heart back. Lord, we are waiting on you.

For Another Brown Boy

As is often the case, I think first of my baby brother, the only brown boy to steal my heart simply by being alive. Once, he lay on our kitchen floor and asked to be taught to read; when our mother tired of reaching for his book, he demanded that this education come by me – and yes, he is a man now. No more little boy begging for his big sister to show him the wonders of the world. To explain the gruesome selfishness of wanting to hold him tight while an entire city loses itself in the street. But if these arms could save only one, he would be my one. And no, I am not fool enough to believe these arms can save him.

Years later, it is no more kitchen table, but wall-to-wall desks for me and my students – a classroom sanctuary for thirty lost boys, most of them left to their own devices until they are old enough for real prison work. Tyshawn with sharp tongue and calculator eyes is two strikes in to his last chance, and I teach him how to be still. How to excuse Malachi for his windbreaker laugh – the joy in himself he's just beginning to see, even while learning to be quiet. How to "yes sir" and smile and stand up straight; to forgive his mother for seeing through him. Mali – his father for not seeing him at all. I have taught them the best I know how to move beneath their brown boy façades. How to take care and remain care free when they are target by virtue of their breathing.

As is often the case, I think next of those lost in the wind. Of Malcolm. Ramarley. Niles. Amadou. Oscar. Sean. Kimani. Eric. Michael. Wendell. The countless unseen, unheard, unknown, unarmed lost souls I have pledged would not be forgotten.

When they speak of this in the teachers' lounge, they will

mention first the riot. How the grief of a people is no longer valid if it comes at the end of a fist. They will point to the perception of violence, the smash and grab, the tear-gassed confusion. They will not say Michael. They will not say murder. they will not say shot down like a dog at the end of its leash – his body left in the midday sun like the pavement were somehow a poplar tree. They will say colorblind. Perhaps inevitable. They will mention the names of the boys in my classroom, and wonder who will be next.

As is often the case, I think last of my older brother, the first brown boy to hold my heart as carefully as his own. Once, he taught me to steel my spine and look a bully square in the face. That there was no need to ever back down with him ready to war on my side – and yes, he is starting a family now. The news keeps showing us countless reasons to fear what has yet to be, but yes, I wish him sons. I wish them a lifetime of peace in the holy of their skin. I have already pledged the whole of my body as barricade if it comes to it. And no, I am not fool enough to believe that will be sufficient.

If the body on the street is ever a boy who somehow belongs to me, there will be no code of law to temper the fire of my anguish. There will be calls for blood as long as the call for justice goes unanswered. There will never be a day I do not paint the city with his name.

The bodies of all these brown boys beautiful will always belong to me.

#LeslieSappIII
#RonSneed
#HashimHanifIbnAbdulRasheed
#OmarrJulianMaximillianJackson
#ArtagoDamonHoward
#MarcusGolden
#MarioJordan
#DonteSowell
#KavondaEarlPayton
#TerenceWalker
#DewayneCarr
#IsaacHolmes
#TianoMeton
#DemarisTurner
#DarinHutchins
#JermonteFletcher
#EdwardDonnellBright
#LedariusDWilliams
#YuvetteHenderson
#DewayneDeshawnWard
#JeremyLett
#JimmyRayRobinsonJr
#MarkellAtkins
#HerbertHill
#JamesAllen
#DesmondLuster
#AnthonyBess
#PhillipWatkins
#LavallHall
#JanishaFonville

#StanleyLamarGrant
#DouglasHarris
#A'DonteWashington
#GlennLewis
#ThomasAllen
#CorneliusJParker
#IanSherrod
#CharlyLeundeuKeunang
#ShaquilleBarrow
#FednelRhinvil
#TyroneRyersonLawrence
#NaeschylusVinzant
#AndrewAnthonyWilliams
#TonyRobinson
#MoniqueJeneeDeckard
#CedrickLamontBishop
#AnthonyHill
#JamieCroom
#TheodoreJohnson
#TerryGarnettJr
#BobbyGross
#KendreAlston
#BrandonJones
#RichardWhite
#DenzelBrown
#DevinGates
#WalterJBrownIII
#NicholasThomas
#JeremyLorenzaKelly
#JamalisHall

#MeganHockaday
#AngeloWest
#ByronHerbert
#MyaHall
#RobertWashington
#DarrinLangford
#EricHarris
#JustusHowell
#WalterScott
#PaulAnderson
#DesmondWillis
#DexterPernellBethea
#DonSmith
#MackLong
#ColbyRobinson
#TevinBarkley
#DanteNoble
#FrankShephard
#JeffreyKemp
#ThaddeusMcCarroll
#DanielWolfe
#WilliamChapman
#ReginaldMcGregor
#ToddJamalDye
#DavidFelix
#TerranceKellom
#JaredJohnson
#AlexiaChristian
#JeffreyAdkins
#EltonSimpson

#BrendonGlenn
#NephiArriguin
#DedrickMarshall
#SamHolmes
#LionelLorenzoYoung
#KelvinGoldston
#D'AngeloStallworth
#RonellWade
#AnthonyGomez
#ChrislonTalbott
#MarcusWheeler
#JavorisWashington
#JeromeCaldwell
#CasoJackson
#AnthonyBriggs
#DaltonBranch
#JamesStrong
#KennethDothard
#KevinAllen
#UsaamahRahim
#DemouriaHogg
#QuanDavierHicks
#IsiahHampton
#CharlesZiegler
#FritzSevere
#DengManyoun
#KrisJackson
#TrepierreHummons
#AlfontishCockerham
#TyroneHarris

#DamienAHarrell
#SpencerMcCain
#KevinLamontJudson
#VictorEmanuelLarosa
#RobertElandoMalone
#KawanzaBeaty
#JasonHendley
#MarcellusJamarcusBurley
#TremaineDantzler
#MarticeMilliner
#JavonHawkins
#FreddieBlue
#EugeneMcSwain
#SalvadoEllswood
#FrederickFarmer
#ChacarionAvant
#AnthonieSmith
#EdwardFosterIII
#AlbertJosephDavis
#DarriusStewart
#SamuelDuBose
#AndreDontrellWilliams
#DevonGuisherd
#DontaeLMartin
#BryanKeithDay
#EarlJackson
#KhariWestly
#AntonioClements
#DariusDGraves
#RaymondHodge

#KeshawnDominiqueHargrove
#CharlesBertram
#ChristianTaylor
#TsombeClark
#DerrickLeeHunt
#ShamirTerrelPalmer
#AndreGreen
#NathanielWilks
#RedelJones
#ReginaldMarshall
#GarlandTyree
#AsshamsPharoahManley
#AllenMatthewBaker
#BenjaminPeterAshley
#FrederickRoy
#MansurBallBey
#DeviereErnelRansom
#ThaddeusFaison
#BobbyTroledgeNorris
#CurtisSmith
#BertrandDavis
#YonasAlehegne
#FelixKumi
#JamesMarcusBrown
#CedricMauriceWilliams
#La'vanteTrevonBiggs
#AngeloDelanoPerry
#IndiaKager
#MohamedIbrahim
#TyroneHolman

#BrandonFoy
#CliffordButler
#JosephThompsonJohnsonShanks
#TyroneBass
#BobbyRAnderson
#DanteOsborne
#KeithHarrisonMcLeod
#JeremyMcDole
#JamesAnderson
#AnthonyMcKinney
#JuniorProsper
#BrandonLamarJohnson
#JefferyMcCallum
#CharlesAPettit
#GaryCarmonaBoitano
#BernardBrandonPowers
#JasonDay
#LesliePortis
#KalebAlexander
#MartinRyansJr
#RickyJaventaBall
#DequanWilliams
#CoreyJones
#DionLamontRamirez
#LamontezJones
#LawrenceGreen
#AdrieneJamarrLudd
#RollyThomas
#DominicHutchinson
#KevinBrunson

#MarqueshaMcMillan
#TyrieCuyler
#AnthonyAshford
#JerryMichaelGrahamJr
#DeaunteLamarBell
#TonyBerry
#BennieLeeTignor
#JamesCovington
#JohnAllen
#DelvinSimmons
#RyanQuinnMartin
#MoisesNero
#RichardPerkins
#ShaneWhitehead
#JamarClark
#YohansLeon
#DemetriusBryant
#JerayChatham
#CorneliusBrown
#MarcusMeridy
#RandyAllenSmith
#SteveDormil
#DarickNapper
#NathanielHarrisPickett
#FreddyBaez
#DariusSmith
#MarioWoods
#RaymoneMDavis
#CarlumandarloZaramo
#MiguelEspinal

#DerekStokes
#CharlesEdwardRosemond
#ChristopherGoodlow
#JavarioShanteEagle
#NicholasRobertson
#CalvinMcKinnis
#RonnieDuboseCarter
#TrayvonScruggs
#LeroyBrowning
#BobbyDaniels
#MichaelNoel
#ChanLeith
#KevinMatthews
#TerrozzaTyreeGriffin
#DaquanAntonioWestbrook
#BettieJones
#QuintonioLeGrier
#KeithChildress
#GermontaWallace
#EricJohnSenegal
#RodneyTurner
#CarltonAntonioMurphy
#RakeemBentley
#HenryBennett
#CraytonWest
#TimothyAlbert
#CedricNorris
#JohnathanBratcher
#JanetWilson
#ChristopherKalonji

#RandolphMcClain
#ChristopherMichaelDew
#CharlesMSmith
#BruceKelley
#PeterJohn
#AntronieScott
#MareseVCollins
#ShalamarLonger
#DavidJoseph
#EricHarris
#MohamedBarry
#PeterFanfan
#SahlahRidgeway
#CalvinSmith
#AliEisaAbdallaYahia
#CalinRoquemore
#DyzhawnLPerkins
#PaulGaston
#MarcosPerea
#CheTaylor
#KishaMichael
#MarquintanSandlin
#TravisStevenson
#ChristopherJDavis
#GregGunn
#CedricFord
#KionteDeseanSpencer
#AkielDenkins
#ArteairPorterJr
#TyrePrivott

#PeterGaines
#MarcoLoud
#KeithMontgomeryJr
#JacaiColson
#LamarHarris
#ScottBennett
#ChristopherNelms
#IndiaBeaty
#ThurmanReynolds
#RobertDentmond
#AlexioAllen
#DominiqueSilva
#JermonSeals
#DerianteDeonMiller
#JamesCraigSimpson
#KimaniJohnson
#MatthewVincentWood
#JamesBrownIII
#CameronGover
#KevinHicks
#LarondaSweatt
#DazionFlenaugh
#LamontGulley
#DiahloGrant
#QuronWilliams
#PierreLoury
#RodneyWatts
#KishaArrone
#RichardBardJr
#GeorgeTillman

#EdsonThevenin
#RicoDonRaeJohnson
#DemetriusDorsey
#JorevisScruggs
#DemarcusSemer
#WillieTillman
#JoshuaBrooks
#KendardelRosario
#AshtianBarnes
#CharlinCharles
#ReginaldDarnellDogan
#BurtJohnson
#DereshaArmstrong
#RonaldDWilliams
#AltonFitzgeraldWitchard
#LionelGibson
#ArthurRWilliams
#JaffortSmith
#ArthurDaRosa
#SeanRyanMondragon
#JabrilRobinson
#JessicaNelsonWilliams
#KentrillWilliamCarraway
#JoshuaBeebee
#MichaelEugeneWilsonJr
#VernellBing
#DollPierreLouis
#DevonteGates
#DennisHudson
#OseeCalix

#MichaelJohnson
#WillieDemetriusJames
#RodneyRodriguezSmith
#DemarcoRhymes
#HenryGreen
#WillisNWalker
#JohnMichaelBrisco
#KeithBursey
#LyndariusCortezWitherspoon
#JohnWilliams
#MichaelMoore
#AntwunShumpert
#RashaunLloyd
#RaufealMBostick
#IsaiahCore
#QuencezolaMauriceSplunge
#DeravisCaineRogers
#JayAnderson
#AngeloBrown
#IsmaelMiranda
#GermichaelKennedy
#DonteLJohnson
#ShermanEvans
#TyroneReado
#LafayetteEvans
#KawmeDejuanPatrick
#JaiLateefSolveigWilliams
#SidneyWashington
#AltonSterling
#PhilandoCastile

#EarnestFells
#AndreJohnson
#AlvaBurnettBraziel
#JosephMann
#JasonBrooks
#OrvilleEdwards
#DaytenErnestHarper
#JermaineJohnson
#GavinEugeneLong
#DerekLove
#AustinJerryLeeHoward
#BernardWells
#JeffCornellTyson
#RichardRisher
#DevonMartes
#DalvinHollins
#JeffreySmith
#PaulO'Neal
#DonnellThompson
#KorrynGaines
#DeMarcoNewman
#JamarionRashadRobinson
#JawariPorter
#EarlPinckney
#DarnellWicker
#SylvilleSmith
#KenneyWatkins
#ColbyFriday
#OmerIsmailAli
#KelleyBrandonForte

#DontaTaylor
#JaqwanJuliusTerry
#LevoniaRiggins
#MichaelThompson
#JeromeDamon
#MosesRuben
#RobertLeeBrown
#SadiqBisharaAbakerIdris
#GregoryFrazier
#TerrenceSterling
#MarkellBivins
#TyreKing
#TerenceCrutcher
#NicholasGlenn
#PhilipHasan
#KeithLamontScott
#OddisBernardColvin
#AlfredOlango
#ChristopherSowell
#GeorgeRichardsMeyers
#DouglasMarrickusRainey
#NajierSalaam
#JacquariusMRobinson
#CarnellSnell
#DonteTJones
#LarryDanielMatthews
#ChristopherDarnellShackleford
#DericJBrown
#KirkFigueroa
#DariusWimberly

#DeborahDanner
#DemetriusMacMoore
#AaronMarquisBallard
#RoyLeeRichards
#MalcolmLorenHickson
#ThadDemarcoHale
#JasonKing
#TerrenceColeman
#MichelleLeeShirley
#FergusonLaurent
#DarrylChisholm
#RasheemSingletary
#SamsonFleurant
#DontrellMontreseCarter
#DariusJones
#EricksonBrito
#GeorgeBushIII
#IvoryCPantallion
#FrankNathanielClark
#TalifScudder
#KajuanRaye
#CleothaMitchell
#JeromeChrisHarmon
#RichardGrimes
#TerrellWalker
#IrecasValentine
#DavidKCrosbyDowdy
#BruceRandallZeusJohnson
#NormanGary
#MarkAnthonyHicks

#RedrickJevonBatiste
#WaltkiWilliams
#KennethRobledo
#LavarMontrayDouglas
#EarlLabonEubanks
#RyanJoseph
#AnthonyLovellEddington
#TerrenceThomas
#DaquanAntonioWestbrook
#GeraldHall
#JamalRollins
#TrevonJohnson
#JamesELewis
#MarkGuirguis
#JamesOwens
#RubenRandolph
#JamalParks
#JRWilliams
#DavionHenderson
#DarrionBarnhill
#JahlireNicholson
#HerbertJohnson
#RonnieLeeShorter
#ChristopherThompkins
#ArmondBrown

As of January 27, 2017, 505 Black men and women have been murdered extrajudicially by United States police officers. Most of their murderers have faced no repercussion. Many of their deaths have gone without mention. But silence will not save us.

We will remember.
We will #SayTheirNames.

#StigmaFree

I have to believe that caring for myself is not self-indulgent. Caring for myself is an act of survival.

Lost Keys and Expired Prescriptions

When she asks if I know I am overreacting,
the things with which I wish to respond
are not youngest daughter appropriate.

I think:
You the one took me to the doctor as a girl,
had him sum up all my IQ points.
Told you the scribbles in my notebook
were equations
and not white noise.
You said 'genius' and 'gifted' to all of your girlfriends
years before there were programs to contain me;
of course I know this heart of mine
is a cacophony of mistakes.

No one of sound self would allow themselves broken
over anything small enough to fit into pocket;
yet here I am
inside out and shattered,
triggered and raw like a trauma victim.
Even the word, 'overreaction' is fresh straw to this camel back:
Today is not one for small things
Today only proves what we don't talk about will always show up in the morning.

How genius is disease presenting itself on the upswing of my pendulum thoughts,
and the crash an inexorable opposite to a rock bottom relentless.
To know a thing,
has never had much to do with how I treat it –
not in a world of polar opposites
and a family of positive spin.

'Gifted daughter'
is an easier story to tell than 'sick one;'
so we stick to that script in conversation even in those
amongst ourselves.

Yes, I know I am overreacting,
is the correct answer to a pointless question,
when the truth is:
My keys are missing,
and I still want to die.

Diagnosis

When everything you know
about who you are
turns out to be a symptom
of some disease,
do not panic;
write your name on the wall.

When reality begins to slip
through your fingers
like broken glass wishing
it were already sand,
return to the wall;
say,
"This is my name.
I wrote it when I could remember
how it sounded in my mother's throat,
and that knowing alone
was reason enough to breathe."

When reason fades into distance,
make a list of the people that love you;
carry it always in your front pocket
with a lighter and some loose change.

When days
turn to weeks,
turn to "My God, it's been so long,"
find a fountain;
make ashes of your list.
Toss them in with a few coins;
make a wish.

Say,
"I swear,

there is a difference between
my name and this disease."
Out loud.
Until you mean it.

Breathe.

This is Not a Suicide Note

tell my father how much i loved being him in this brand new body
that the barrel laugh and crooked smile will always call me home
how i tried not to hold anyone tight enough to break them
that the shatter was inevitable
i tried to sweep up all the pieces
tell him i know these hearts get heavy
that i understand the leaving
that i am a master of running away
tell the boy with the eyes like unanswered prayers i am learning the rules of forgiveness
that i stopped handing out any second chances
i am sure i will need to cash them in
i know a thing about folding
i know a bit more about going all in
about ruthless and reckless and not looking back
i admit
i have been my own pillar of salt
but far less than i have been my own mountain
tell god he will have to deal with my mother
answer for all the broken promises
tell her that being all knowing will sometimes leave you without all the facts
that black holes are the unfortunate result of having to look away
i do not turn from impending crash
i run headlong to the panic
tell the girl with the bottomless ribcage
i am sorry for all of the panic
i am sorry for every time the apology came too late
this is not an apology
this is not regret
this is not a suicide note

tell the skyline i am grateful for all the days i found it open
and how this city is another name for heaven's welcome mat
tell the sky
i know it's hard to handle all the stardust
that it is worth its weight in water
that it is doings its best with the smoke
that the horizon is a crooked smile belting out its barrel laugh
this is not a suicide note
i am coming home

Commendation

The Southeastern Order of Thrown-Away Dishes commends you for years of deliberate service. For afternoons spent at the superstore – frantically searching for pots and spoons to replace what you would not clean. For that which you have discarded. We have noticed what you deem disposable. We have seen you consider yourself. We have seen you stand, near immobile, recalling every move you have made. Diligence is not the problem. You, so committed to this heart you carry, it is easy to mistake work for worth – and so, some things are thrown away.

Do you remember the time a full sink, then receipt, sent you broken to the kitchen floor? How you wept on the tile for hours? How you did not return to work for one week? It has been years since then. We have seen you grow stronger. These days, you are paper plates in the trash, and the same cookware for one year. We have seen you wrestle with seeing the intrinsic value of keeping things. We have seen you consider yourself. Do not give up until you find it.

Today

The front door is dead-bolted.
The screen is latched.
The couch is covered with last night's clothes.
The trash is full, but there is no garbage out of and around
or beside it.
The lamp is off; the books away;
the kitchen a quiet hum of refrigerator noise,
and there are no sad poems today.

There was a homeless man just at the corner
with a plaid shirt and misspelled sign.
He smiled almost ten dollars' worth for the five and change
I gave him.
I did not offer him a place on the couch or a meal from the
fridge,
but I locked the door –
thinking of the gray and shrivel –
tuning out the voice in my head that says he should be
welcome here.

Hearing voices is not a symptom
often saddled with this disease.
The myth of energy enough to change the world at 1:00am
still is.
I tell myself I cannot cure hunger.
I tell myself not to empty the fridge.
I tell myself the man is most likely an angel, who finds
himself fallen from grace.
The only known cure for falling is teaching yourself to get
back up –
to heave yourself on unsteady feet even if you are alone.

There should be a poem about being alone,
but there are no sad poems today.

Not when there's money after the bills and a meal planned for tomorrow.
Clean clothes. Made bed.
A door that will not greet me ajar first thing the next morning when all of my strength is bidding me breathe.
Praise the tiny victory.
Praise the thing for which no one knows I will always struggle.
The grind of day-to-day and how there is still some fight in me.
Even when the fight is just keeping the car on the road.
Coming home to sink void of dishes.
Being thankful that guardian angels are willing to work for smiles and spare change.

The front door is locked.
I am warm and full.
There are no sad poems today.

#Epilogue

none of the words will ever compare to
how it feels to cross the savannah – at
sunrise or sunset when either direction is
heading towards home. it is the only place
i've fallen in love and watched a man die
beneath a velvet midnight when we were
too young to stand still. a river like that will
always hold you – how it moves and goes
nowhere – the water a more sincere music
than the falsetto of your blood. and there
are too many poems about water; too many
poems about blood; too many poems about
the moonlight and the things we were ashamed
to do beneath it. but a few miles down from
the bridge that we call a highway is another,
smaller bridge built from softer, smaller hands -
ones that knew every story starts with a solid
place to jump from. we meet there a few times
a year with a list of things we should say goodbye
to and remember what it meant to be young
and fearless and somehow still afraid. there
are no words for a moment like that – with
the water and stone beneath you- the
stars laid in a jewelry box I still call my own;
i fell in love here once. many years ago.
haven't tumbled that way since, but i know
the mouth of this river. how it always says,
welcome home.

CPSIA information can be obtained
at www.ICGtesting.com
Printed in the USA
BVHW020225150419
545498BV00003B/24/P

9 780692 813980